Concerning Violence

Concerning Violence

Fanon, Film,
and Liberation in Africa,
Selected Takes 1965–1987

Edited by Göran Hugo Olsson and Sophie Vuković

This edition published in 2017 by
Haymarket Books
P.O. Box 180165
Chicago, IL 60618
773-583-7884
www.haymarketbooks.org
info@haymarketbooks.org

ISBN: 978-1-60846-532-3

Trade distribution:
In the US, Consortium Book Sales and Distribution, www.cbsd.com
In Canada, Publishers Group Canada, www.pgcbooks.ca
In the UK, Turnaround Publisher Services, www.turnaround-uk.com
All other countries, Publishers Group Worldwide, www.pgw.com

This book was published with the generous support of Lannan
Foundation and Wallace Action Fund.

Cover design by Rachel Cohen. Cover image from film still by Lennart
Malmer.

Printed in Canada by union labor.

Library of Congress Cataloging-in-Publication data is available.

10 9 8 7 6 5 4 3 2 1

Contents

Introduction

Göran Hugo Olsson, Sophie Vuković,
and Joslyn Barnes

We started working on the *Concerning Violence* film in 2012, two years before Eric Garner was choked to death by a violent New York City police officer. Garner's last desperate gasp, accompanied by the words "I can't breathe," was caught on video camera and later amplified by protestors in the streets of New York carrying posters with the image of the Afro-Caribbean psychiatrist, philosopher, and revolutionary Frantz Fanon and his statement, "We revolt simply because, for many reasons, we can no longer breathe."

From New York and Ferguson, Missouri, to Iraq, Syria, Afghanistan, Mali, and beyond, Fanon's masterwork *The Wretched of the Earth*—written more than fifty years ago—offers us a path for understanding and conceivably *ending* the violence that is shaping the experience and existence of a majority of people on our shared planet.

Of course our planet is not equally or equitably shared, and that realization—that colonization is not dead, but rather transformed into an extractive, militarized, global corporatocracy—is what drove us to revisit Fanon's work in the first place. To understand the neo-imperialism prevalent today—the violence of it and the violence that breaks out as a response to it—we needed to explore the roots of the contemporary situation. As Europeans and Americans working with Fanon's ideas, we needed to explore the hypocrisies of our own European and US liberal democracies, which declare that they oppose violence and consider colonialism a thing of the past and yet marshal, subcontract, or outsource violence to preserve their purportedly humanist exceptionalism. The result is the film *Concerning Violence*, inspired by and an adaptation of *The Wretched of the Earth*.

Fanon's devastatingly astute and prescient political analysis of the process of decolonization and the fate of a "postcolonial" world is complemented by his perspective as a psychiatrist who dedicated his life to healing the victims of colonial violence and simultaneously understood violence as a passage through the destroyed self toward life. In effect, Fanon offers us a way out of hell, by walking us through it.

Working with the Text

No one has illustrated the complexity of anticolonial struggles as clearly and poetically as Frantz Fanon. As filmmakers, our challenge was to bring Fanon's words to life onscreen and to turn a nonfiction book into a cinematic experience. Mindful that audiences are immersed in the pace and rhythm of a film while viewing it—which differs greatly from the experience of readers moving through a book at their own pace—we worked throughout the editing process to present the text as dynamically as possible. But we also needed the text to resonate with audiences who live in a world that has changed immensely since 1961, when the book was written, and address the changes in our relationship to both text and image and the viewing experience of film itself. The text that appears in the film *Concerning Violence* and in the book you hold in your hands is excerpted and edited, some of it having been translated by us from the original French.

In our text selection process, we tried to use the book's structure to guide us, but we ended up making selections solely from the first and last chapters: "Concerning Violence" and "Conclusion." We made this decision because the text in these chapters is more direct, expressive, and dynamic than in the main body of the book where Fanon goes into detail about and focuses on specific political and historical events in various countries to make his arguments. We wanted to allow the *footage* to unfold and serve this function for the viewer instead. So to accompany our film chapters, we selected text that was more philosophical or broadly descriptive of structural mechanisms that could be applied to various scenarios in the struggle for liberation from colonial rule.

One of our challenges was discerning how to simplify and modify the more academic phrasings and sections to make them work as a film script. Out of respect for Fanon, we were hesitant to take liberties with rewording and rearranging the text. Yet the film is transparent about being an adaptation of *The Wretched of the Earth*, and we wanted to keep the feel and tone of the text as intact as possible. We felt that the text needed at times to be updated for a contemporary audience. Examples of this included the persistent use of male pronouns or the word "man" as a stand-in for the more universal "humankind" or "person," the gendering of Europe as female, references to the "yellow races," and other outdated phrasings. We felt these linguistic practices would be grating to the ears of a contemporary audience, so we revised Fanon's phrasing in some instances while at the same time maintained some of the original language, even in its outdatedness.

The process of weaving together a script for the film from *The Wretched of the Earth* took nearly two years. The fusion of the Fanon text and the archival images was a process of collaboration with our master film editors—Michael Aaglund and Dino Jonsäter—and was ongoing until picture lock.

Formally, the text is written in an urgent, poetic, and unapologetic tone—it demands that you stop and listen. Indeed, *The Wretched of the Earth* was not actually "written" so much as it was dictated by Fanon to his wife and friends while he suffered from late-stage leukemia and failing eyesight caused by the disease. His conclusion is a jeremiad by comparison to the more academic approach of its opening chapters—a characteristic Ms. Lauryn Hill channeled in her performance of the narration.

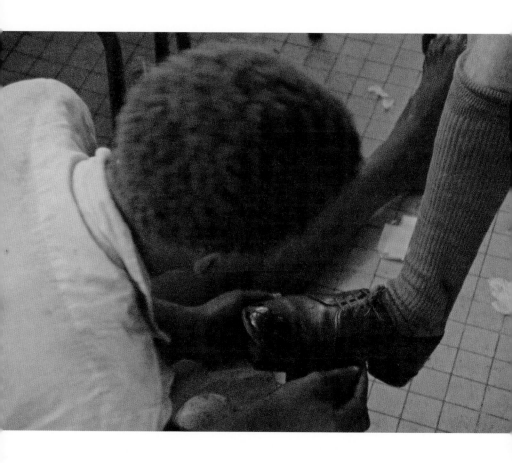

The Film's Preface:
Professor Gayatri Chakravorty Spivak

We decided early on that we wanted to include a cinematic preface to the film to both situate Fanon for a contemporary audience and address the original book preface by Jean-Paul Sartre, whose controversial interpretation had the effect of both widening the audience for *The Wretched of the Earth* and exercising great influence on how it has come to be understood—or misunderstood.

Few thinkers have offered such an uncompromising and sharp analysis of colonialism and its legacy or of the globalized twenty-first century as Gayatri Chakravorty Spivak. Happily, she accepted our invitation to lend her brilliance to our effort and succeeded—in one stunning take—to create a preface for the film that builds a bridge between the historical period depicted in the archival footage and today, and between the circumstances that shaped Fanon's words and the ever-expanding violence that limns our contemporary political horizon. She also adds a crucial gender dimension to the masculinist stance of both Sartre and Fanon.

This stance is not confined to the texts; it is also found in the archival footage. And while we managed to find gems—for example, female FRELIMO commanders in Mozambique—women are largely excluded in the footage showing anticolonial freedom struggles, even though we know they had a major role in these struggles. In touching upon this fact, as well as the continuation of gendered violence in all conflicts throughout history and today, Spivak gives the audience tools with which to read and interpret both what is shown in the film and what is not shown.

Lastly, she also critiques the film, in an elegant and (possibly) accurate way, which we found refreshing because—as a great teacher will—she encourages you to think for yourself.

The Graphics

The sheer number of images that deluge us can dull our awareness, so we chose to use Fanon's text to interrupt the image—at times offering a cinematic encounter with the text that also reinforces the narrative voice. This karaoke-style narration was something we developed early on in the filmmaking process and was realized by our artistic director, Stefania Malmsten. Apart from adding an interesting aesthetic to the film frame, we noticed that it was easier for viewers to take in and understand the text being read if they could also see it.

Some parts of Fanon's text really land better when they are both visually and aurally expressed. Other words have a poetic and flowing pace that sounds more like a friend talking directly to you, and in those parts we chose not to include graphics. We did not make up rules for how to edit the graphics, but in every frame we worked intuitively to get the right balance among the words, the voice, the images, and the graphics in order to best serve that part of the story.

The Voice

The experience of the film is very reliant on the voice that carries the text. Through our mutual friend Corey Smith, who produced the music on our previous film, *The Black Power Mixtape: 1967–1975*, we knew that Ms. Lauryn Hill was a big fan of Frantz Fanon. As she was in jail for tax problems, she was reachable only by post. So we wrote her a letter with some of the text we were editing and examples of images, explaining the idea of the film. She immediately responded by telling us how unbelievable it was for her to receive this request, since she was spending evenings in her cell studying Fanon. She wrote, "I will not just do the voice—I want to do the music as well." Unfortunately, there was not enough time between her release and the premiere of the film for her to record and edit the music. But true to her word, Ms. Hill was released from jail on a Friday, and the following Monday morning she went into a studio and recorded the entire script in approximately forty minutes.

It was a fantastic experience to hear the text for the first time in her interpretation. We had been working with a dummy recording for over a year and knew the text was not easy to read or record. The last work by the dying Fanon, the text sprawls out in many different directions. That is the beauty of it, but it makes it terribly difficult to read. Ms. Hill had no problem whatsoever. The text ran like water through our speakers.

But there was a problem: her pace was way too fast for a film voiceover—it was simply too fast to use as narration for the whole film. She was okay with re-recording; however, the pace was still too fast, the result, we guessed, of the up-tempo style of her music at the time. So we had to go back to Ms. Hill and ask for yet another recording, which was not easy for us, due to our respect for her artistry. We see her as one of the great artists of our time.

She responded by noting that reading this text had released four hundred years of oppression for her and that this meant that the text had become a celebration. And a celebration, she explained, is always up-tempo. She compared it to when Charlie Parker and John Coltrane discovered the African roots in jazz and created be-bop—which is also up-tempo.

We had no argument with this, but we still needed to get a slower reading. In a book you can read at your own chosen tempo, going back and forth in the text, and with a song you can play it many times over. But in a film theater the audience is inside the experience of image, sound, time, and space—and if you lose them, it takes time to get them into the film again. Ms. Hill gracefully responded: "But people will see this film many, many times." Nonetheless, she assented to doing the reading more slowly. And it was beautiful.

Ms. Hill's voice adds a dimension that a filmmaker can only dream of: the tone, intonation, and rhythm of this iconic artist, along with her deep comprehension of the text, are what make this film what it is. Once you've heard it, it's almost impossible to imagine the film without it. It imprints on your consciousness. And in making additional versions of the film in eight different languages so far, we have striven to find other brilliant artists who can lend their gifts to this work. They include Gael García Bernal in Spanish, Shima Niavarani in Swedish, and the legendary actress Kati Outinen in Finnish. More will follow.

The Footage

One of the most frequently asked questions we get wherever we screen the film (as of now, in twenty countries via theatrical release and more than a hundred film festivals) is about the footage. It is truly amazing that all the footage was broadcast on Swedish national television between 1966 and 1986, and more than 90 percent of it was produced by Swedish filmmakers and reporters. That's a story in itself.

The earliest footage from the archive is the beautiful black-and-white film made about the Swedish mining company LAMCO in Liberia. This film *Svart vecka i Nimba,* made by Roland Hjelte, Lars Hjelm, and Ingrid Dahlberg, was intended as a celebration of the Swedish export industry's success in Africa. However, when the filmmakers arrived at the mine, a strike had erupted and they shifted the object of the film's focus from the biggest Swedish foreign investment at that time to the oppression of the mine workers and the denial of their rights.

The Swedish management at LAMCO was very naïve, and in participating with the film crew they were transparent and actually helped the filmmakers expose the prison-camp conditions of the mine. When it was broadcast, the film was a total blow to the big powers in the Swedish economic sector. And for the first time they realized that public television could be a critical voice and a potential danger. It was a rude awakening, especially for the Wallenberg family, which owned the mine in Liberia and was—and still is—the most powerful industrial family in Sweden.

After that, there was a constant stream of filmmakers going to Africa, most famously to portray the liberation movements. This was fuelled by solidarity with the struggles against imperialism—especially during the war in Vietnam—but was also made possible by Sweden's "neutral" stance during this peak of the Cold War. It was also a very rich country and had the resources to help fund its filmmakers. Therefore, it was decided that Swedes should report to their compatriots about the outside world, rather than relying on foreign media—especially foreign media from NATO or, even worse, Warsaw Pact countries.

Also, due to Sweden's history of supporting the African National Congress in South Africa from the early '50s and Dr. Martin Luther King Jr. and the civil rights movement in the United States, Swedish filmmakers could more easily gain access to and establish a rapport with the various liberation movements in Africa. Despite Sweden's shameful historical and significant role in the transatlantic slave trade, Swedes were not looked upon as colonizers as the French, British, or Portuguese in Africa were at the time, but rather more as allies with an understanding of the ongoing struggles.

By far the most important filmmakers who contributed to the imagery of *Concerning Violence* are Lennart Malmer and Ingela Romare, whose magnificent scenes in the film include those shot in Mozambique and Guinea-Bissau, where they had established personal relationships with Amílcar Cabral and other leaders. Members of the first batch of students out of the newly opened Swedish film school, they made an unbelievable number of significant films in Africa and also in Vietnam, the United States, and Northern Ireland during a ten-year period.

It's crucial to note that the images that make up *Concerning Violence* are not from a newsfeed or stock footage. They come from documentaries that are artfully made in their own right, and that's why the images are so strong. They are not just about capturing something on film; they are about both encountering and allowing a human story to unfold in a cinematic form.

We hope their inclusion, together with all the efforts made and gifts offered by the people who collaborated to make this film, will serve the larger challenge that Fanon put forth: to set afoot a new human being and, perhaps, a different future. And that depends on every one of us.

Preface
Professor Gayatri Chakravorty Spivak

rantz Fanon was born on the Caribbean island of Martinique in 1925 and grew up a young gentleman of the French Empire. He realized, when he came from the island of Martinique to the mainland of France in Europe, through involvement in De Gaulle's Free French army in Algeria earlier, that his class standing among his own black people did not mean anything in the country of the colonizing masters—he was nothing but a black man. In a famous chapter in his book *Black Skin, White Masks* (rejected as a dissertation by a French university), he mentions his shock when a white French child cries out to her mother: "Mama, see the Negro!" But Fanon moves from just this shock into an attempt to understand colonization all over the world. In this very book, in the last chapter, he walks us through a reading of the European philosopher Hegel's famous chapter "Master and Slave" and turns it to his own use. As we watch the film *Concerning Violence*, we remember this in the freedom fighters' invocation of the named states of Mozambique and Angola, borders established by the imperialists. Fanon's lesson was that you use what the masters have developed and turn it around in the interests of those who have been enslaved or colonized. In this he is with great leaders like W. E. B. Du Bois and Nelson Mandela. Fanon did not stop at thinking colonization, as he wanted to do something about it. He gave his time and skill to the healing of those who suffered from violence. He was placed in Algeria in North Africa, an African country that spoke French—as the resisters in this film speak Portuguese—creolizing the master's language as their very own. Such thinking is shared by great writers such as Assia Djebar of Algeria, Njabulo Ndebele of South Africa, and Syed Abdul Malik of India. As a trained psychiatrist, working in the Blida-Joinville Psychiatric Hospital and developing a radical theory of colonial psychopathology, he helped those who fought against French colonialism with the FLN, the National Liberation Front of Algeria, joining the party himself in 1954. My friend Assia Djebar, whom I have already mentioned, worked with him in Tunisia and has shared with me in detail the actual experience of his work—to heal the effects of violence, rather than to condone violence as such.

Fanon died at thirty-six, and we would have gained greatly if this man of fire and resolution had lived long enough to give us his wisdom when the colonized nations regularly fell into internal violence and internal class struggle and internal greed after so-called liberation. The issue of colonization is a greed shared by humankind. No one is better than anyone, every generation must be trained in the practice of freedom, caring for others, as did Fanon, and that is what colonization stops. Within the greed for capital formation, colonization allows already existing ignorant racism to spread the markets in the name of civilization or modernization or globalization, as it does today.

Göran Olsson's film is nested as a moment in *The Wretched of the Earth,* the book Fanon wrote in the last ten weeks of his life, knowing that he was marked for death by acute leukemia, even as he was being hounded by the colonizing government of France.[1] The French philosopher Jean-Paul Sartre, himself a strong anticolonialist among the colonizers, probably only read the powerful first chapter, and read it as an endorsement of violence itself—not reading between the lines. We are acquainted with the well-meaning hyperbole of reverse ethnocentrism, where Fanon insists that the tragedy is that the very poor—among the peasantry untamed by bourgeois socialization—is reduced to violence, because there is no other response possible to an absolute absence of response and an absolute exercise of legitimized violence from the colonizers. Their lives count as nothing against the death of the colonizers: unacknowledged Hiroshimas over against sentimentalized 9/11s. Here the lesson of Gandhi regarding the power of passive resistance and the contrastive lesson of Israel in the exercise of state-legitimized violence drawing forth violence in extremism is useful today. It captures the tragedy of the moment when the very poor are convinced, in the name of a nation that is going to reject it once it is established on its own two feet, to offer themselves up for a violent killing.

---

1. Frantz Fanon, *The Wretched of the Earth,* trans. Richard Philcox (New York: Grove, 2004). Quotations in text marked with page numbers in parentheses.

Indeed, if one reads the book carefully to the end, one sees that Fanon's discussion of violence is drawn from the cases that he encounters in his clinic. He understands the reason with sympathy, but does not give an endorsement. His role is to investigate the difficulties of the cure.

It is in this context that we remember that after the struggle against Portugal, the new nations of Angola and Mozambique fell into civil war and disproved the dream of the very poor that decolonization would bring a new day. Mozambique has joined forces with capitalist globalization. This is the rule rather than the exception. Fanon's own warning is contained in *A Dying Colonialism*. Against the grain of his optimism of the will, he writes: "It is no longer the age of little vanguards," an unintended description of the guerrilla warfare we will watch on the screen.[2] Working within the problems created by a postcolonial nation (which bring back the precolonial problems that the great historian Fernand Braudel called *longue durée* or long term): "structures which lie invisible below the surface of social activities," many of us think that the real disaster in colonialism lies in destroying the minds of the colonized and forcing them to accept mere violence—allowing no practice of freedom, so that these minds cannot build when apparent decolonization has been achieved.[3] From the example of mature leaders such as Du Bois and Mandela, we know or can at least have the feeling that Fanon would have gone in that direction. Unlike Gandhi, the early Du Bois, or even Mandela, who worked for their own nation-states—Fanon was not himself an Algerian, not a member of the country which he helped. This is an important lesson for those of us who want to think the world rather than

---

2. Frantz Fanon, *A Dying Colonialism*, trans. Haakon Chevalier (New York: Grove, 1965), 1.

3. This is the accessible summary of Braudel's argument offered by one of his best pupils, Kirti N. Chaudhuri, in *Asia Before Europe: Economy and Civilisation of the Indian Ocean from the Rise of Islam to 1750* (New York: Cambridge University Press, 1990), 5.

thinking from within a nation-state, argue from identity, learning the lesson that mere national liberation without the practice of freedom cannot in fact bring a socially just world for the very poor. Fanon did not know the language of the common people of Algeria—Arabic; he was not himself a Muslim, the majority religion of Algeria. He could not know the power of religion as a discourse of political mobilization in today's world, particularly after so-called independence in what is today called "the Islamic world." I was working the election booths in Wahran (Algeria) in 1991. It is within the context of the aftermath of colonialism—that Fanon could not know but predicted with great accuracy—that the tragedy of what we watch in this film must be carefully considered. This is a teaching text.

Indeed, if we go back to the later sections of *The Wretched of the Earth*, especially "The Trials and Tribulations [*Mésaventures*] of National Consciousness," we see how Fanon discusses the return of the structures that preexisted colonialism in terms of the failure of Pan Africanism in postcoloniality.

In this brief compass, I will not touch his discussion of sub-Saharan Africa, the idea of North Africa as the white Mediterranean, the contrasting idea of the Arab invasion, and the broad comparisons he made with Latin America. I will confine myself to commenting on his uncanny description of Angola and Mozambique as they are today: neopatrimonial, one-party states, complicit in capitalist globalization, manipulating the structures of so-called democracy in order to continue the status quo. I quote a few sentences from his amazingly prescient description:

> The ministers, chiefs of cabinets, the ambassadors, the prefects are chosen from the ethnic group of the leader, sometimes even directly from his family. Regimes of such familial types seem to take up again old laws of endogamy and one experiences not anger but shame in the face of this stupidity, of this imposture, of this intellectual and spiritual misery. These heads of state are the true enemies of Africa because they sell it to the most terrible of its enemies: stupidity. (225)

Indeed, he comments again and again—in the repetitive structure of that tortured book, written in the last ten weeks of his life, facing a painful death—on how to deal with nation-state boundaries in globality. There are contradictions here. On the one hand, there is the middle-of-the-road injunction to end the Cold War, on the other hand there is the "revolutionary" exhortation to get rid of the old nationalist bourgeoisie; all through there is the strong subalternist initiative of recognizing that the first surge of anticolonialism is not nationalist among the peasantry. The most eloquent and sustained hope is that young people will be trained to citizenship by transforming the meaning of "politicization":

> The greatest task is to understand at all moments what is happening with us. We must not cultivate the exceptional, look for heroes, another form of the leader. We must lift the people, expand the brain of the people, furnish it, differentiate it, make it human, . . . To be responsible in an underdeveloped country is to know that everything depends definitively on the education of the masses, on the elevation of thought, of what one calls too quickly: politicization. (239)

It is our task to reinscribe this innocent anti-imperialist gendered auto-critical humanism; as in Du Bois and Gramsci, to recognize that this is altogether different from the Fanon who was understood to have said only that violence for decolonization will bring in a new world. Such were indeed the last words of the book, but that peroration is given the lie by the intervening chapters, after "Concerning Violence." I want rather to endorse the Fanon who wants us to think about the negotiations between the various imperial systems, the last item on my list. This is the Fanon who mentions Latin America again and again, for Algeria was not yet postcolonial when he died.

Du Bois should be mentioned here as well because he was sentient enough to distinguish between the various kinds of imperialisms that were afloat at the time, in an essay published in the year of Fanon's birth (1925).[4] I do a work that can be situated within the thinking of

---

4. W. E. B. Du Bois, "The Negro Mind Looks Out," in Alain Locke, ed., *The New*

the Fanon–Du Bois style of Pan-Africanism that also wanted to bring within its embrace the vision of a postcolonial world at large, Fanon looking forward into globality.

Preparing to finish my piece on the film for publication, I have been reading a history of Mozambique in connection with the fact that the archives represented in the film are Angola and Mozambique. What do I find but India's involvement, by way of Portuguese Goa, in the development of Mozambique as a part of new Iberia, negotiating with the older Arab presence and the constant subaltern movement, and finally into a neo-patrimonial postcoloniality. A certain work of cultural gendering has to be confronted here as Chinese women from the Portuguese possession of Macao were being brought in since European and Indian women were refusing to come and settle in this wild country.

We must account for Mozambican and Angolan nationalism as a product of what Fanon calls an alliance between the nationalist professionals and the soft colonialists. "The masses" echo but are not a part of it. This is why the state of Independence, writes Fanon, becomes "semi-colonial" (213). With this in mind, we listen to the boy in the film, as he speaks so movingly about his desire to be a medical doctor, witness to what Fanon calls the separation between the nationalists and the masses. We must note with sympathy how the US-based revolutionary leader Eduardo Mondiane, assassinated in 1969, re-describes that "wildness": "by the fifteenth century, highly organized and materially advanced Bantu-states had grown up, states which were responsible for settlements like the great stone city of Zimbabwe."[5] The lovely singing and dancing in the film footage can then be understood as a culturalist replication in a time of anticolonial war.

I end, as usual, with the question of gender.

We remember that Fanon wanted very much to consider the rep-

Negro (New York: Touchstone, 1925), 385–414.

5. Eduardo Mondiane, *The Struggle for Mozambique* (Baltimore, MD: Penguin, 1969), 16.

resentation of the veiled woman and the revolutionary unveiled woman in his *Sociologie d'une revolution*, translated as *A Dying Colonialism*. Because he was doing this in connection with the kinds of patients he saw as a psychiatrist trying for a new anticolonial psychiatry, single-issue feminists have often misunderstood him. However, it is also true that his sexual politics were marked by time and place. But the words of this wild boy from Martinique can still find an echo because, in the radiation of globality, below a certain class, rape-culture is still taken to be as normal as bribe-culture. In the classes above they are mostly hidden by benevolent sexism with a smile. And the response to no-response in certain parts of the world has been gender-envy, an insistence on women as culture-bearers—even as we speak, groups want to bind women in Sharia, which must not be translated as "law," as Wael Hallaq explains in his "What Is Sharia?" but rather classed with this gender-envy.[6]

This film reminds us that, although liberation struggles force women into an apparent equality—starting with the nineteenth century or even earlier—when the dust settles, the so-called postcolonial nation goes back to the invisible long-term structures of gendering. The most moving shot of this film is the black Venus, reminding us of the Venus of Milo with her arm gone, who is also a black Madonna, suckling a child with bare breasts. This icon must remind us all that the endorsement of rape continues not only in war but also, irrespective of whether a nation is developing or developed—in women fighting in legitimized armies. Colonizer and colonized are united in the violence of gendering, which often celebrates motherhood with genuine pathos. Here we have to promote our brother Fanon into a changed mindset, but he, who would have been in his eighties today, is not there for us. What I can recommend is that you also watch a video made by Algerian women active in the revolution called *Barberousse ma soeur*, if you can get your hands on it; or read Assia Djebar's

---

6. Wael Hallaq, *Shari'a: Theory, Practice, Transformations* (New York: Cambridge University Press, 2009).

representation of the glorification of the mother in *Regard interdit, son coupé,* translated as "Forbidden Gaze, Severed Sound."[7]

Here now is our film, a tribute to and an illustration of Frantz Fanon's *Wretched of the Earth.* I end this preface in Fanon's own way, turning around for our own use what a European philosopher wrote for the use of Europe over two hundred years ago; turning Kant around for our purposes as he did Hegel: "Anything which the people (i.e., the entire mass of subjects) cannot decide for themselves and their fellows cannot be decided for the people by the sovereign either." The people under colonization have had no practice of freedom. You cannot decide without practice. The ones you see on the screen are a small part of the people, the poorest of the poor, mobilized into violence by sovereign leaders: cannon fodder. This practice goes on in all armies, all resistance movements, in the name of nation and religion. Here Fanon would have been useful today. As for gendering, we must ourselves gender "the people." Our brothers Kant and Fanon are not useful here, although we must keep in mind that Fanon put his finger on the fact that, even in contemporary globalization, gender justice produces the alibi for development as exploitation. When we look at negotiations between imperial systems, this particular feature is often not noticed.

I thank Göran Olsson for setting us these tasks.

---

7. Assia Djebar, "Forbidden Gaze, Severed Sound," in *Women of Algiers in Their Apartment,* trans. Marjolijn de Jager (Charlottesville: University Press of Virginia, 1992), 133–52.

COLONIALISM IS NOT A THINKING MACHINE, nor a body endowed with reasoning faculties. It is violence in its natural state, and it will only yield when confronted with greater violence. . . .

National liberation, national renaissance, the restoration of nationhood to the people . . . whatever may be the headings used or the new formulas introduced, decolonization is always a violent phenomenon. . . .

Decolonization . . . is a historical process. . . . It cannot be understood, it cannot become . . . clear to itself except by the movements which give it historical form and content. . . .

Decolonization, which sets out to change the order of the world, is, obviously, a program of complete disorder. But it cannot come as a result of magical practices, nor of a natural shock, nor of a friendly understanding.

—Frantz Fanon

Colonialism is not a thinking
machine, nor a body endowed
with reasoning faculties.

It is violence in its natural state,
and it will only yield when
confronted with greater violence.

Chapter One

Decolonization

With the MPLA in Angola, 1973

The Portuguese colonies were the last to be liberated in Africa. In Angola, several entities were fighting the Portuguese army, backed by NATO (North Atlantic Treaty Organization). Of these, Movimento Popular de Libertação de Angola (Popular Movement for the Liberation of Angola), popularly known as the MPLA, was the biggest, led by the slum doctor and poet Agostinho Neto and supported by Cuba and the Soviet Union. Rival group UNITA (União Nacional para a Independência Total de Angola, National Union for the Total Independence of Angola) was led by Jonas Savimbi and was backed by South Africa, the United States, Great Britain, and China.

After liberation from Portugal in 1975, Angola was thrown into Africa's longest civil war, between the MPLA and UNITA, which ended with the death of Jonas Savimbi some twenty years later. Cuban involvement peaked in the biggest tank battle on African soil since World War II at Cuito Cuanavale in 1987, where forty thousand Cuban troops defeated a South African–led invasion. Nelson Mandela called it "an important step in the struggle to free the continent—and our country—of the scourge of apartheid" and noted, "The decisive defeat of the aggressive apartheid forces destroyed the myth of the invincibility of the white oppressor."[1]

—Editors' Note

---

1. Nelson Mandela, address for the opening of the National Moncada Barracks, Havana, July 26, 1991, Latin American Network Information Center, Castro Speech Data Base, http://lanic.utexas.edu/project/castro/db/1991/19910726-1.html.

Gaetano Pagano Reports on the MPLA in Angola, 1973

REPORTER GAETANO PAGANO: On the night of the 23rd of May, I was taken by MPLA into Cambinda near the Congo border. And there preparations were being made for this military operation. Cambinda contains one of the world's largest oil deposits, larger than Kuwait. They carried more than 40, up to 50 kilos each because they had to carry their own ammunition plus the ammunition for the twenty bazookas in the force. They walked very swiftly anyway, using mainly tennis shoes or light rubber shoes.

After these several days of march, we finally came close to the Portuguese base and camped in the forest within about 2.5 kilometers of the base. The reconnaissance commander Max explained the situation of the base and how the attack was to be carried out. We moved from the camp about three o'clock in the morning, and everything was done in great calm and absolute silence. And as soon as it became light enough just to barely see, the order was given to open fire. They only fired back for a couple of minutes with machine guns; after that there was no reaction on their part anymore. Very soon many buildings in the base started burning. There was a big explosion in an ammunition depot.

When the attack was stopped, a small group of MPLA came out of the base with a Jeep. If I've ever seen a guerrilla movement that is like a fish in the water, well, that's MPLA in Cambinda. I've seen it with my own eyes.

YOU DO NOT TURN ANY SOCIETY, however primitive it may be, upside down with such a program if you have not decided from the very beginning to overcome all the obstacles that you will come across in so doing.

The native who decides to put the program into practice, and to become its moving force, is ready for violence at all times. From birth it is clear to him that this narrow world, strewn with prohibitions, can only be called in question by absolute violence.

Decolonization is the meeting of two forces, opposed to each other by their very nature. Their first encounter was marked by violence and their existence together—that is to say the exploitation of the native by the settler—was carried on by the impact of a great array of bayonets and cannons. . . .

In decolonization, there is therefore the need of a complete calling into question of the colonial situation. If we wish to describe it precisely, we might find it in the well-known words: "The last shall be first and the first last." Decolonization is the putting into practice of this sentence. That is why, at a descriptive level, all decolonization is successful.

The naked truth of decolonization evokes for us the searing bullets and bloodstained knives which emanate from it. For if the last shall be first, this will only come to pass after a murderous and decisive struggle between the two protagonists. That affirmed intention, to place the last at the head of things, can only triumph if we use all means to turn the scale, including, of course, that of violence.

—Frantz Fanon

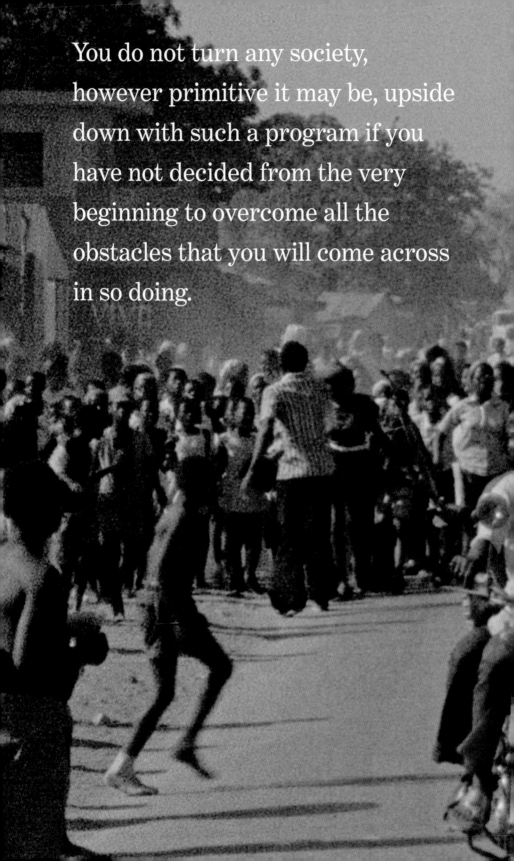

You do not turn any society, however primitive it may be, upside down with such a program if you have not decided from the very beginning to overcome all the obstacles that you will come across in so doing.

The native who decides to put
the program into practice, and to
become its moving force, is ready for
violence at all times. From birth it is
clear to him that this narrow world,
strewn with prohibitions, can only
be called in question by absolute
violence.

Decolonization is the meeting of two forces, opposed to each other by their very nature. Their first encounter was marked by violence and their existence

together—that is to say the exploitation of the native by the settler—was carried on by the impact of a great array of bayonets and cannons.

Chapter Two
Indifference

This interview with Tonderai Makoni (later known as Simba Makoni) was part of a half-hour show on political prisoners and torture called *Fokus,* shown on national broadcast in Sweden in 1970. The show was produced in collaboration with Amnesty International and featured testimonials by people from South Africa, Nepal, the United Kingdom, and Poland. Dr. Makoni returned after the fall of the Ian Smith regime in Rhodesia and became Zimbabwe's minister of industry and energy at only thirty-one years old. He much later became the minister of finance but has since been part of the political opposition to Robert Mugabe, and ran an election campaign in 2008 for president, finishing third.

—Editors' Note

Interview with Tonderai Makoni, PhD, Dissident in Sweden, 1969

TONDERAI MAKONI: I heard a rough knock on the door. I say, "Who is there?" and they shout, "Police!" So I dressed up and went with police to police cells. They told my wife that I'll be back in a short period of time.

REPORTER: How long were you in prison?

MAKONI: I was in prison approximately for five years.

REPORTER: Could you tell me how it affects you?

MAKONI: Well, when I was in detention the feelings I had, and my colleagues had, I look at it as the history of black people. From the days of slavery. I found out they suffered in the hands of white people. Then I looked at the days of colonialism. I also found out that black man was again at the bottom of everything, under oppression from white man. Then I looked at America and Britain. And I found out despite the emancipation, the black man was still at the bottom of everything. He is as an object. And then we look at South Africa and Rhodesia. We find out these are the countries with institutionalized racism. Where again black person is at the bottom of everything. And of course torture is something less than human. He is an object.

If you don't tell them what they want, you then go to detention. But the other system of torture is that they tie your legs to a tree, your hands to a car—and pull. They say if you don't tell us who did what or what you did, we are going to pull you apart. And of course they pull. Some people have died as result of torture.

The other system of torture is that they get a plastic bag. With an elastic band which they cover your head with. If you are covered in a plastic bag for a period of time, you just shoot up in the air and drop. And when you drop. If it break or doesn't break. You will bleed in your ears and mouth and nose. So it's very terrible.

REPORTER: What did you feel when you came out of prison?

MAKONI: I've grown in a way to feel indifferent. The torture that I've gone through for . . . [the] last five years made me less and less feeling about things. Just take life as it comes. So even when I came out there was no great excitement on my part. And I felt that I was still in prison.

Chapter Three
Rhodesia

Formerly part of the British Crown colony of Southern Rhodesia, the self-declared and unrecognized state of Rhodesia existed from 1965 to 1979 and modeled itself on South Africa. There had been attempts to overthrow white minority rule in Rhodesia since the early 1960s, which were cruelly suppressed by the white minority government. But by 1966, African nationalist forces led by "the Patriotic Front," a union between Joshua Nkomo's ZAPU (Zimbabwe African People's Union) and Robert Mugabe's ZANU (Zimbabwe African National Union) had armed themselves with support from the Soviet Union and the People's Republic of China and posed an undeniable threat to the minority white ruling population.

Under the rule of Ian Smith, a prime minister intent on fighting for a "whiter, brighter Rhodesia," the white minority was determined to maintain power and fought back in the "Bush War," or "Second Chimurenga" as it was called by the guerrillas. However, after the Portuguese withdrew from Mozambique in 1975, both Rhodesia and its only ally South Africa seemed less confident of a victory—considering that the black-to-white ratio of the population was twenty-two to one. By the time a peace agreement was brokered in 1979 (with help from then UK prime minister Margaret Thatcher), the remaining white minority could no longer deny the majority support for the new nationalist parties.

—Editors' Note

Interview with an Unidentified Rhodesian Settler

UNIDENTIFIED RHODESIAN SETTLER (to employee who is serving drinks): Thank you, Timothy. But you didn't open that one, you stupid thing, you. But no bother. We'll open it ourselves.

REPORTER: Did you always believe that one day you would leave Rhodesia?

SETTLER: Never ever. No, I was one of the guys who were gonna stay here and switch off the lights and return. I was gonna switch off the lights and then close the gates and say, "Right, Rhodesia: farewell," and then burn as we go back. And that didn't happen. I was gonna switch off the lights and return, but things are happening so fast at the moment it's just, I haven't got that much time anymore.

REPORTER: You're going and leaving the lights on?

SETTLER: That's right, somebody else'll have to switch them off.

REPORTER: Why don't you stay and take the gamble? Take the risk?

SETTLER: But there is no risk; I mean, there is no gamble. There is a risk, but there's no gamble. The gamble is all in the . . . the gooks have got it.

REPORTER: The who?

SETTLER: The gooks. The terrorists. The whole world, the whole world is supporting the terrorists.

REPORTER: Has the attitude of Africans changed as a result of what is currently happening?

SETTLER: Yes.

REPORTER: In what way?

SETTLER: I've got a staff, the company I work with, has got a staff of about eight Africans. And they all think they're going to own houses. I've never seen so many Africans driving, learning to drive motorcars, as I have lately because every one of them thinks they're going to get a motorcar. A little garden—we call him a "garden boy"—was washing my mother-in-law's car. And he said to her, "Well, next year, that's going to be my car." So my mother-in-law went to him and said, "You see this box of matches and this lighter? I'll burn it before I give it to you." So that's the attitude of the Africans; it's changed completely.

The ratios here at the moment, I think we are about thirty-four to one, maybe a bit more, with everybody taking a gap like me. In South Africa at the moment, I think it's about four to one. I think, about four to one. So you could stand a chance.

REPORTER: Does that make you feel happier?

SETTLER: Well, I could take out four Affies before they take me out.

REPORTER: But you couldn't thirty-six?

SETTLER: No way, Jose.

Interview with Robert Mugabe, 1974

INTERVIEWER: What is your general attitude towards the white minority, if they remain in the country?

MUGABE: We accept them. Every white man who would like to remain in the country is free to do so.

Provided he accept the system, that will be established. The new government, of course. He must accept that his privileges based on color have gone. He will not have a different set of privileges from those which are accorded to members of other racial groups. But overly, we will not perpetuate the system where people are organized communally on the basis of race or color. We want an integrated society where not the color of the person counts but the skill he is able to show, and the contribution he is prepared to make to the development of the country.

Chapter Four

A World Cut in Two

L eading up to the end of the "Bush War" at the end of the 1970s, a mass exodus of the minority white population in Rhodesia was being prepared with help from the South African government. A border crossing point was secured and refugee camps for displaced white Rhodesians was created. In 1980, an internationally supervised democratic election was held, and the (at the time) self-professed Marxist Robert Mugabe and his ZANU Party won with a clear majority. After this, many white families prepared themselves to leave the country.

Although they were not colonies, Rhodesia and South Africa were the two biggest countries that applied an independent minority rule, that is, white supremacy, through monopoly over natural resources and also through oppressive violence—in South Africa known as apartheid. Not only was the political and economic structure monopolized to benefit whites, but the entire countries were planned and designed to facilitate total segregation. All roads, highways, and railroads had the double function of being both modes of transport and airtight borders between people. In South Africa this is still in full effect, the most obvious example being Cape Town, where communities still have difficulties leaving their "section" because of logistic, economical, and cultural barriers.

—Editors' Note

In the colonies it is the policeman and the soldier who are the official, instituted go-betweens, the spokesmen of the settler and his rule of oppression.

THE COLONIAL WORLD IS A WORLD CUT IN TWO.

The dividing line, the frontiers, are shown by barracks and police stations. In the colonies it is the policeman and the soldier who are the official, instituted go-betweens, the spokesmen of the settler and his rule of oppression. . . .

The intermediary does not lighten the oppression . . . [but] puts [it] into practice with the clear conscience of an upholder of the peace; yet he is the bringer of violence into the home and into the mind of the native.

The zone where the natives live is not complementary to the zone inhabited by the settlers. The two zones are opposed, but not in the service of a higher unity. . . .

The settlers' town is a strongly built town, all made of stone

The colonial world

and steel. It is a brightly lit town; the streets are covered with asphalt, and the garbage cans swallow all the leavings, unseen, unknown and hardly thought about. The settler's feet are never visible. . . . His feet are protected by strong shoes, although the streets of his town are clean and even, with no holes or stones.

. . .

The town belonging to the colonized people, . . . [the shanty town] the Negro village, the medina, the reservation, is a place of ill fame, peopled by men of evil repute. They are born there, it matters little where or how; they die there, it matters not where, nor how.

It is a world without spaciousness; men live there on top of each other, and their huts are built one on top of the other. The native town is a hungry town, starved of bread, of

is a world cut in two.

meat, of shoes, of coal, of light. The native town is a crouching village, a town on its knees, a town wallowing in the mire. It is a town of niggers and dirty Arabs.

The look that the native turns on the settler's town is a look of lust, a look of envy; it expresses his dreams of possession—all manner of possession: to sit at the settler's table, to sleep in the settler's bed, with his wife if possible.

The colonized man is an envious man. And this the settler knows very well; when their glances meet he ascertains bitterly, always on the defensive, "They want to take our place." It is true, for there is no native who does not dream at least once a day of setting himself up in the settler's place.

—Frantz Fanon

The town belonging to the colonized people, . . . [the shanty town] the Negro village, the medina, the reservation, is a place of ill fame, peopled by men of evil repute. They are born there, it matters little where or how; they die there, it matters not where, nor how.

Chapter Five

LAMCO, Liberia, 1966

LAMCO was one of the biggest enterprises of the Swedish mining industry to directly exploit iron ore mining outside Sweden and Sápmi, the indigenous part of Sweden. The footage in this chapter comes from the film *Black Week in Nimba* by Roland Hjelte, Ingrid Dahlberg, and Lars Hjelm, which aired on Swedish television in 1966. It shocked the industrial sector in Sweden, in particular the most prominent Swedish business family, the Wallenbergs, who operated LAMCO.

In a Cinéma vérité style and in interviews, the film tells the story of how the company utilized the national army to end a strike aiming to achieve gains to meet the most basic needs of the workers. Never before had the public broadcast service critiqued or exposed in a negative way the economic sector like this. The film led to an inflamed debate on the role of the Swedish Broadcast Company and journalists in general that would continue well into the 1980s—and it led to the labeling of public television as a leftist entity, with an agenda of obstructing "free" enterprise. The CEO of LAMCO, Olle Wijkström, who with a naïve sincerity exposed the attitude of the company toward the workers on film, felt misunderstood and wrote several articles and books defending himself and LAMCO. But in the public eye, LAMCO became the symbol of how Swedish companies abroad gave up their principles of collaboration with the unions and the workers that had made them so successful in Sweden.

—Editors' Note

LAMCO, Liberia, 1966   59

A Strike at LAMCO in Liberia, 1966

LAMCO REPRESENTATIVE: July 27, 1966. Your employment has now ceased to exist. And you have to leave the company house you are occupying and the occasions area house from July 28, 1966.

ROBERT JACKSON: See that?

LAMCO REPRESENTATIVE: The company will provide transportation to the boundary of the consensual area for you.

JACKSON: Never mind. I get a copy, you get a copy, that's alright.

I'll take this matter to the federal department. There's no signature line, they would tell me "sign here." I'm not so stupid. Listen, let me tell you something. I was about to go to work. You understand? But now, I have to get some kind of information from Mr. Goody.

SWEDISH OFFICIAL/WHITE-COLLAR: No, no. No information. You sign this copy, or you leave it.

SWEDISH REPORTER ROLAND HJELTE: Thursday, the 21st of July of this year. A normal working day. But today, soldiers are posted at the workplace. The work is down. The Liberians in Nimba have gone on strike.

The chairman of the trade union at LAMCO. Jailed and accused of having led a few thousand Liberians to demonstrate for higher pay, a strike which was declared illegal before it began.

He awaits his fate outside the mess hall in Nimba. Here, the leaders of the union are led to cars by the LAMCO management. Here are representatives of the Liberian government, who have already disclosed the journey's destination: the notorious prison Belle Yella, infamous for being the country's worst torture prison, from whence few, if any, return.

SWEDISH CEO OF LAMCO, MR. WIJKSTRÖM: In our opinion, the trade

union's management has behaved in a completely irresponsible and illegal way. There is a trade union law that regulates the rules of the game between employers and employees. And it's been totally broken. At 7 a.m. in the morning, everything was still calm. The workers went to a meeting at the trade union instead of to work. On Monday morning, military reinforcements arrive from Monrovia. A battalion of three hundred men gathers outside the officers' mess hall. After formation, they load up their sharp ammunition.

UNNAMED UNIONIST/FORMER LAMCO WORKER #1: Are you going to tell me that if the workers in Sweden strike or something like that, you think the government is going to use arms on them?

No. We're not violent, nobody uttered no words of violence, neither any threat.

HJELTE: Why are the soldiers here then?

UNNAMED UNIONIST/FORMER LAMCO WORKER #2: Well, the soldiers

are here on LAMCO's claim or on LAMCO's desire. But there is no threat nor word of violence ever been used to anybody. A strike was not even organized by the chairman; it was organized by the workers themselves who were tired and fed up of the LAMCO management who wouldn't pay them the money, so they decided to strike.

HJELTE: The next day, everyone knows about the eviction threats. Yet still, the workers' buses return almost empty. And the trade union building has been surrounded by the military to prevent any further meetings for the strikers.

LIBERIAN PRESIDENT WILLIAM TUBMAN: I wrote them a letter and told them they were violating the laws of the country.

And that they could not strike until they had first submitted grievances. If they had any grievances, they should submit them. First amendment in keeping with the law. And if they could not agree, then refer the matter to government.

But they persisted, and would not go back to work. I then ordered the place to be policed so as to prevent violence.

LOCAL POLICE/MILITARY OFFICER: My orders were to break the mob, or whatever existed, by all costs.

And, of course, if it had become necessary to resort to force. My orders were to fire over people's heads originally, and then wound a few people in the attempt to break the crowd. If this would have been a necessity.

HJELTE: For the LAMCO management, the day was marked by a miscalculation. The strike would not end. They were faced with the risk of having to fire most of their workforce.

WIJKSTRÖM: As it turned out, only 25 percent of them showed up. We thought a larger percentage of workers would come to work, but they did not.

HJELTE: Thursday. A week has passed since the strike broke out. The decision must come today. By seven o'clock in the morning, everything is over. The workers have returned. It now remains for LAMCO to deal out the punishment. Thirty letters of termination are to be handed out. The recipients are those Liberian workers who had already been cast as troublemakers. These thirty troublemakers are sought out in their homes on Thursday morning, but none of them are at home. Even they had returned to work.

JACKSON: My children, they didn't realize anything. I said to them: "Children, I'll tell you one thing: this is not your home." Presently I have five of my children with me [here]. One at home, one at school. One died this year.

WIJKSTRÖM: Robert Jackson wondered why he had been fired. What did his boss, Sören Lagergren, know?

SÖREN LAGERGREN: Tough question, I don't know. But he was a very good guy who surely has a future as a telephone man ahead of him. I don't know anything about why he stopped working here.

HJELTE: So, it wasn't the case that there was something wrong with his efforts?

LAGERGREN: No, definitely not. He was very good. Out of my guys, he is the one who has developed the most. He could go out to work all by himself to do repairs.

JACKSON: When the truck came I put all of my things in, got my family, and put everything in the truck, my boys and myself. We didn't want to go from this place.

HJELTE: After an hour's journey on rough roads, they were finally outside the LAMCO property area, twenty-two miles from Nimba. That day, the eviction cars traveled like a shuttle service. The way the driver was driving . . .

JACKSON: I even advised him: I said, there's a woman here with us, my brother-in-law's wife, she was in the car and she was pregnant. I said, "Take your time." Still, the driver wouldn't hear me. I said, if anything happens then, okay it's on you.

HJELTE: The truck stops in the middle of the bush. Robert Jackson's five-year employment with LAMCO is definitely over. One detail remains: a receipt of the journey here. "This is to certify that the officers transported my belongings and my family without any damages or accidents, Robert Jackson."

The soldiers had done their job. In the dark, Robert Jackson and his family were left to manage on their own. The previous strike had resulted in a pay raise, which enabled the workers to buy a meal during their workday. There had been cases of workers falling asleep during their shift because they had not eaten.

This strike gave the workers nothing.

WHEN YOU EXAMINE AT CLOSE QUARTERS the colonial context, it is evident that what defines one's place in the world is the fact of belonging to or not belonging to a given race, a given species.

In the colonies the economic substructure is also a superstructure. The cause is the consequence; you are rich because you are white, you are white because you are rich.

—Frantz Fanon

LAMCO, Liberia, 1966   65

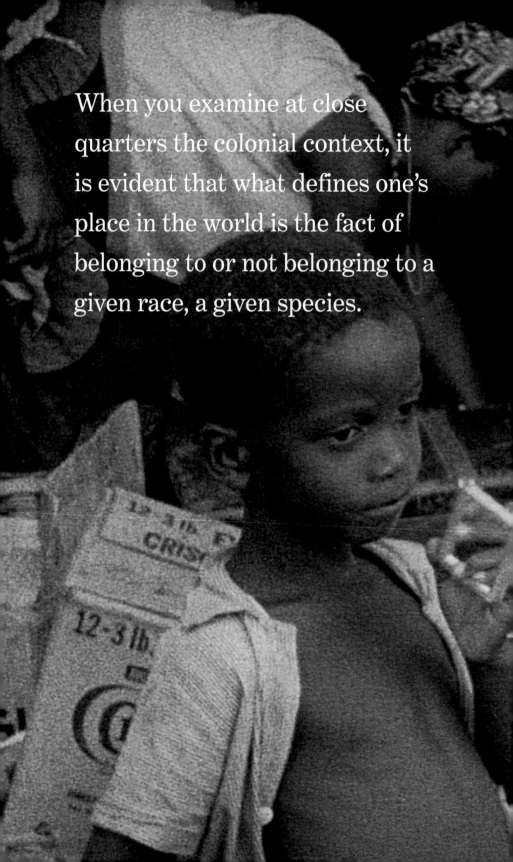

When you examine at close quarters the colonial context, it is evident that what defines one's place in the world is the fact of belonging to or not belonging to a given race, a given species.

In the colonies the economic substructure is also a superstructure. The cause is the consequence; you are rich because you are white, you are white because you are rich.

Chapter Six

That Poverty of Spirit

C hristian missionaries played a major role in colonization around the world. Here we see a Swedish film that exposes the dynamics of naïveté and ignorance, in this case with a Swedish couple posing in front of local people working to build their church. Sweden has a long and strong tradition of sending missionaries to Africa, and still today, a large proportion of Swedish churches are also engaged in supporting various Christian activities and organizations in Africa. This sequence is from the 1969 film *White Ants* by Bo Bjelfvenstam and Jörgen Persson.

—Editors' Note

NATIVE SOCIETY IS NOT SIMPLY described as a society lacking in values. . . . The native is declared insensible to ethics; he represents not only the absence of values, but also the negation of values. . . .

All values, in fact, are irrevocably poisoned and diseased as soon as they are allowed in contact with the colonized race. The customs of the colonized people, their traditions, their myths—above all, their myths—are the very sign of that poverty of spirit. . . . As soon as the native begins to . . . cause anxiety to the settler, he is handed over to well-meaning souls who . . . point out to him the . . . wealth of Western values.

I speak of the Christian religion, and no one need be astonished. The Church in the colonies is the white people's Church, the foreigner's Church. She does not call the native to God's ways but to the ways of the white man, of the master, of the oppressor. And as we know, in this matter many are called but few chosen.

—Frantz Fanon

Native society is not simply
described as a society lacking in
values. . . .

The native is declared insensible
to ethics; he represents not only
the absence of values, but also the
negation of values.

Interview with Two Swedish Missionaries in Moshi, Tanzania, Conducted by Reporter Bo Bjelfvenstam in 1970

REPORTER: How long have you been here?

MALE MISSIONARY: Here in Tanzania? Since '52, in December.

REPORTER: It would be interesting to know what has changed here? The main change?

MALE MISSIONARY: The biggest change is that it became an independent state.

That's actually one of the biggest.

REPORTER: Have the people changed? On the inside, so to speak?

MALE MISSIONARY: They're about the same, I think.

REPORTER: Have you yourselves changed?

MALE MISSIONARY: Yes, one certainly has after so many years.

REPORTER: In which direction?

MALE MISSIONARY: Well . . . one looks at the situation a bit differently now than when one first came out here, I imagine. One sees the situation a bit more realistically, perhaps.

REPORTER: Have you tried to change people? That's been part of your assignment here, hasn't it?

MALE MISSIONARY: Yes, of course. We're here in the service of the mission so in that sense, we have tried to change them.

REPORTER: Primarily, of course, in religious matters?

MALE MISSIONARY: Yes.

REPORTER: What kind of religions existed before you came here? Were there religions you don't approve of, so to speak?

I mean African religions.

MALE MISSIONARY: The African religion . . . what can one say . . . it has always existed, so it continues to exist, of course.

But the mission has gained a very strong hold on the soul of the people.

REPORTER: But this must have meant big changes in many aspects, for example family organization, polygamy, things like that.

MALE MISSIONARY (LOOKING TO FEMALE MISSIONARY): Maybe you can answer that?

FEMALE MISSIONARY: Well, as a mission, we forbid our members to have more than one wife, because in our opinion it causes a lot of suffering for the women, so in the places where the mission has been active for many years, there's been a big change in that issue.

REPORTER: Couldn't it cause even greater suffering for the women, if they suddenly have to divorce their husbands and have no one to take care of them?

FEMALE MISSIONARY: Yes, of course, for those who have already taken a second wife. But it's unthinkable for a member of our congregation to get married for a second or third time. He has to be satisfied with his first wife.

REPORTER: But is that a Christian point of view or a European point of view? Is there support for monogamy in the Bible?

FEMALE MISSIONARY: There is, isn't there?

REPORTER: Is there?

FEMALE MISSIONARY: In the New Testament at least . . .

REPORTER: Does it say somewhere that you can only have one wife?

FEMALE MISSIONARY: It says that a congregation leader should be a one-man wife . . . I mean, a one-wife man.

REPORTER: Oh, really? And now you're building a church here in Moshi.

MALE MISSIONARY: Yes.

REPORTER: Is that what comes first, the church and evangelization?

MALE MISSIONARY: Yes, that's what we try to do.

REPORTER: Will you build schools and hospitals here as well?

MALE MISSIONARY: We don't know yet, but that will come second in any case. But first a church, because we feel a very big need for one.

IN THE COLONIAL CONTEXT, the settler only ends his work of breaking in the native when the latter admits loudly and intelligibly the supremacy of white man's values. . . .

For a colonized people the most essential value, because the most concrete, is first and foremost the land: the land which will bring them bread and, above all, dignity. But this dignity has nothing to do with the dignity of the human individual: for that human individual has never heard tell of it. All that the native has seen in his country is that they can freely arrest him, beat him, starve him: and no professor of ethics, no priest has ever come to be beaten in his place, nor to share their bread with him. As far as the native is concerned, morality is very concrete; it is to silence the settler's defiance, to break his flaunting violence—in a word, to put him out of the picture. The well-known principle that all men are equal will be illustrated in the colonies from the moment that the native claims that he is the equal of the settler.

The native intellectual had learnt from his masters that the individual ought to express himself fully. The colonialist bourgeoisie had hammered into the native's mind . . . the essential qualities of the West: the idea of a society of individuals where each person shuts himself up in his own subjectivity, a society whose only asset is individual thought.

The native's muscles are always tensed. You can't say that he is terrorized, or even apprehensive. He is in fact ready at a moment's notice to exchange the role of the quarry for that of the hunter. The native is an oppressed person whose permanent dream is to become the persecutor. The symbols of social order—the police, the bugle calls in the barracks, military parades and the waving flags—are at one and the same time inhibitory and stimulating: for they do not convey the message "Don't dare to budge"; rather, they cry out "Get ready to attack."

—Frantz Fanon

In the colonial context, the settler only ends his work of breaking in the native when the latter admits loudly and intelligibly the supremacy of the white man's values.

The native intellectual had learnt from his masters that the individual ought to express himself fully. The colonialist bourgeoisie had hammered into the native's mind ... the essential qualities of the West: the idea of a society of individuals where each person shuts himself up in his own subjectivity, a society whose only asset is individual thought.

THE COLONIZED MAN WILL FIRST manifest the aggressiveness which has been deposited in his bones against his own people. This is the period when the niggers beat each other up, and the police and magistrates do not know which way to turn when faced with the astonishing waves of crime.

Where individuals are concerned, a positive negation of common sense is evident. While the settler or the policeman has the right the livelong day to strike the native, to insult him and to make him crawl to them, you will see the native reaching for his knife at the slightest hostile or aggressive glance cast on him by another native; for the last resort of the native is to defend his personality vis-à-vis his brother. Tribal feuds only serve to perpetuate old grudges buried deep in the memory. By throwing himself with all his force into the vendetta, the native tries to persuade himself that colonialism does not exist, that everything is going on as before, that history continues.

It is as if plunging into a fraternal bloodbath allowed them to ignore the obstacle, and to put off until later the choice, nevertheless inevitable, which opens up the question of armed resistance to colonialism. Thus, collective autodestruction in a very concrete form is one of the ways in which the native's muscular tension is set free. All these patterns of conduct are those of the death reflex when faced with danger, a suicidal behavior which proves to the settler that these men are not reasonable human beings.

(In the same way the native manages to bypass the settler. A belief in fatality removes all blame from the oppressor; the cause of misfortunes and of poverty is attributed to God: He is Fate. In this way the individual accepts the disintegration ordained by God, bows down before the settler and his lot, and by a kind of interior restabilization acquires a stony calm. It has always happened in the struggle for freedom that such a people, formerly lost in an imaginary maze, a prey to unspeakable terrors yet happy to lose themselves in a dreamlike torment, such a people becomes unhinged, reorganizes itself, and in blood and tears gives birth to very real and immediate action.)

The oppressor starts the process of domination, of exploitation, and of robbery. In the other sphere the coiled, plundered creature which is the native provides fuel for the process as best he can. The process moves uninterruptedly from the banks of the colonial territory to the palaces and the docks of the mother country. In this becalmed zone the sea has a smooth surface, the palm tree stirs gently in the breeze, the waves lap against the pebbles, and raw materials are ceaselessly transported, justifying the presence of the settler: and all the while the native, bent double, more dead than alive, exists interminably in an unchanging dream.

The settler makes history; his life is an epoch, an Odyssey. He is the absolute beginning: "This land was created by us"; he is the unceasing cause: "If we leave, all is lost, and the country will go back to the Middle Ages."

The native is boxed into a corner; apartheid is simply one form of the division into compartments of the colonial world. The first thing which the native learns is to stay in his place and not to go beyond certain limits.

This is why the dreams of the native are always of muscular prowess; his dreams are of action and of aggression. I dream I am jumping, swimming, running, climbing. I dream that I burst out laughing, that I span a river in one stride, or that I am followed by a flood of motorcars which never catch up with me. During the period of colonization, the native never stops achieving his freedom from nine in the evening until six in the morning.

—Frantz Fanon

The colonized man will first manifest the aggressiveness which has been deposited in his bones against his own people. This is the period when the niggers beat each other up, and the police and magistrates do not know which way to turn when faced with the astonishing waves of crime. All these patterns of conduct are those of the death reflex when faced with danger, a suicidal behavior which proves to the settler that these men are not reasonable human beings.

The oppressor starts the process of domination, of exploitation, and of robbery. In the other sphere the coiled, plundered creature which is the native provides fuel for the process as best he can.

The process moves uninterruptedly
from the banks of the colonial
territory to the palaces and the
docks of the mother country.

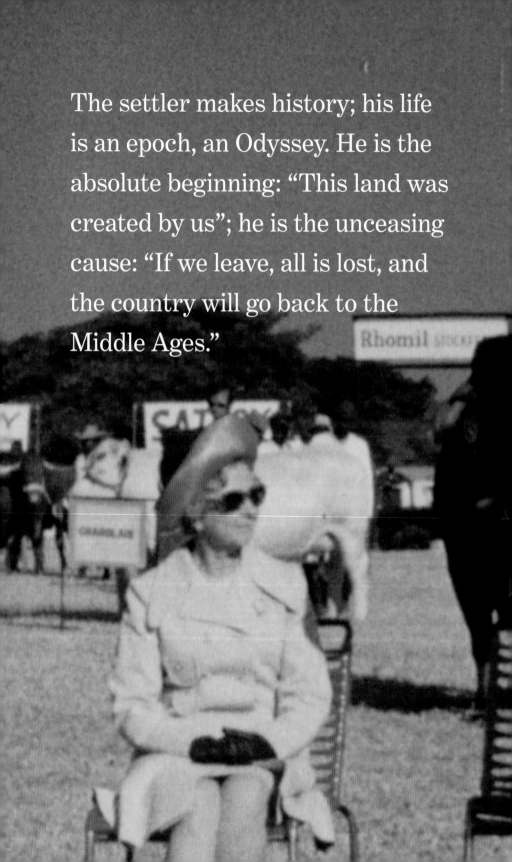

The settler makes history; his life is an epoch, an Odyssey. He is the absolute beginning: "This land was created by us"; he is the unceasing cause: "If we leave, all is lost, and the country will go back to the Middle Ages."

Chapter Seven

The Fiat G.91

With the FRELIMO in Mozambique, 1972

Frente de Libertação de Moçambique (FRELIMO) or the Mozambique Liberation Front was founded in 1962 to organize for liberation from Portugal. From 1964 to 1975 FRELIMO fought for freedom from colonial rule in the Mozambican War of Independence with support from China, the Soviet Union, and the Scandinavian countries, including Sweden. By the late 1960s, FRELIMO had established the "liberated zones" in the north of Mozambique, where FRELIMO instead of the Portuguese colonial government acted as authority. Largely informed by Marxist-Leninist ideology, FRELIMO set up cooperative forms of agriculture and gave the peasant population access to education and health care, in the form of makeshift hospitals and day care centers in the bush. FRELIMO was successful in attracting women to engage in armed struggle against colonial rule, and female commanders enjoyed nearly the same stature and privileges as male commanders. Uniquely, female commanders also commanded male soldiers and not just other female soldiers.

—Editors' Note

Interview with Two Female FRELIMO Military Commanders in Mozambique, 1972

COMMANDER NUMBER 1: We will not go back. The revolution is going forward and we will not return to the past. Our eyes are wide open. We are united over the cause. Our cause is to defend our country. We are happy that these friends have come to visit us and to report on us.

So we are going to sing you a song.

FEMALE FRELIMO MEMBER: We decided to go into the bush because we saw the actions of colonialism. Five hundred years of slavery. We peacefully asked for independence, but they didn't care. They massacred us.

We fled to the bush and took up guns because of the actions of colonialism. I am ready and I am part of the guerrilla.

We want to rule our own destinies as Mozambicans. But now, inside the FRELIMO, we rule ourselves. In the old days no Mozambican would talk to the white people, as I am doing now. Now, the Black Mozambicans call meetings where we decide together.

MALE FRELIMO OFFICER: We can see that the enemy has lately been increasing psychological actions against the population. These psychological actions consist of the massive use of airplanes provided by the NATO countries, namely jet planes such as the Fiat G.91.

Almost constantly, these planes are terrorizing the population and dropping many napalm bombs, which have caused a lot of suffering to the population.

VOICEOVER BY A SWEDISH REPORTER: FRELIMO's guerrilla army doesn't have any air force at its disposal. The Portuguese are in control of the air space; the colonial army can temporarily occupy smaller territories within the liberated zones. The Portuguese can control their artillery and troops to whatever point. For the last three years the Portuguese have only been able to enter the zones by helicopters. When they leave their helicopters and go by foot in the jungle, they become targets for the guerrilla.

They remain no longer than a couple of weeks before they get killed or are driven off. The Portuguese try to destroy as much of the harvests as possible in order to starve out the guerrillas. They terrorize the local population at the attacks, in order to make them feel that the FRELIMO can't protect them. They destroy as much as they can of what the locals have built up. This means that every school, hospital, and orphanage in the liberated zones is a military target for the Portuguese colonial authority.

FEMALE FRELIMO COMMANDER NUMBER 2: In the old days, we could not study. Because of the colonial exploitation, they didn't give us time to study. And without studies, you are dominated. As we didn't study we didn't know what was happening in the world, so we could do nothing and this was the intention of the colonizer. Because of colonialism, our grandparents and our parents could not send us to school. They suffered a lot. Many of us were caught and sent to work on a farm at Mpanga and Mwangane where we were not paid. The very little we received was only enough to buy salt. It wasn't enough to buy clothes

for our children. This was the strategy of the colonizer so they could colonize us even further.

FEMALE FRELIMO COMMANDER NUMBER 1: Since we founded the FRELIMO, we are very happy with the work that has been done for Mozambican women. We are on the same level as men. There are male and female commanders. The heads of the defense department are both male and female. We help each other. There is no difference in rights, we are on the same level. The work the man does, the woman can also do. And vice versa.

SIMÃO ELIAS: My name is Simão Elias. I am with the FRELIMO, as a member of the FRELIMO, to help the people of Mozambique, as I am also from Mozambique. I was born in Mozambique and this is the best thing I can do to help my people. With medicine it is the same thing. I am practicing medicine, so that I can have some good ideas so I can help the health system, to help my people.

REPORTER: When will Mozambique be free?

ELIAS: Mozambique, we don't know when it will be free. . . .
    We just don't know when it will be free.

REPORTER: Do you think the war will last long?

ELIAS: It may last or not, we don't know.

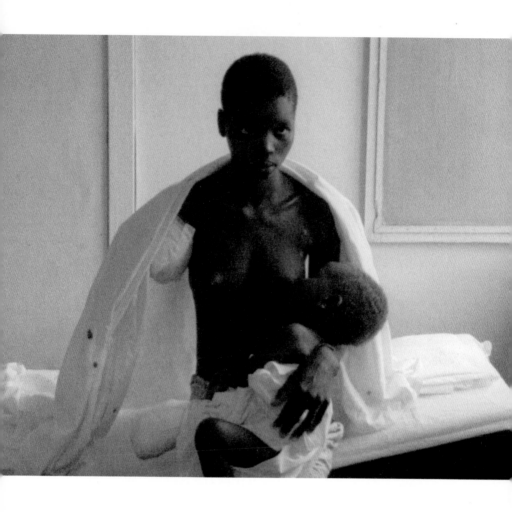

The exploited man sees that his liberation implies the use of all means, and that of force first and foremost.

THE IMMOBILITY TO WHICH THE NATIVE is condemned can only be called into question if the native decides to put an end to the history of colonization—the history of robbery—and to bring into existence the history of the nation—the history of decolonization.

The peasantry is systematically disregarded. And it is clear that in the colonial countries the peasants alone are revolutionary, for they have nothing to lose and everything to gain. The starving peasant, outside the class system, is the first among the exploited to discover that only violence pays. For him there is no compromise, no possible coming to terms; colonization or decolonization is simply a question of relative strength.

The exploited man sees that his liberation implies the use of all means, and that of force first and foremost.

—Frantz Fanon

Chapter Eight
Defeat

After four hundred years of colonial rule in its African colonies, Portugal was the last of the European countries to withdraw, and it did so only after costly and bloody wars of independence. The wars spanned almost two decades, and Portugal, receiving support from NATO, employed terror war tactics against the largely underfinanced guerrilla forces. Similar to US war tactics in Vietnam, the Portuguese bombed civilian targets rather than military ones and used chemical weapons and air strikes on the population.

—Editors' Note

THE COLONIZED MAN FINDS HIS FREEDOM in and through violence. Violence enlightens, because it indicates the means and the end. At the level of individuals, violence is a cleansing force. It frees the native from his inferiority complex. It makes him fearless and restores his self-respect. The mass of the people struggle against the same poverty, flounder about making the same gestures, and with their shrunken bellies outline what has been called the geography of hunger. It is an underdeveloped world, a world inhuman in its poverty; but also it is a world without doctors, without engineers, and without administrators. "If you wish for independence, take it, and starve, and go back to the Middle Ages."

Decolonization never takes place unnoticed, for it influences individuals and modifies them fundamentally. It brings a natural rhythm into existence, introduced by new human beings, and with it a new language and a new humanity.

(When a colonialist country, embarrassed by the claims for independence made by a colony, proclaims to nationalistic leaders "If you wish for independence, take it, and go back to the Middle Ages," the newly independent people tend to acquiesce and accept the challenge; in fact you may see colonialism withdrawing its capital and its technicians setting up around the young state the apparatus of economic pressure. The apotheosis of independence is transformed into the curse of independence, and the colonial power through its immense resources of coercion condemns the young nation to regression. A regime of austerity is imposed on these starving men. An autarkic regime is set up and each state, with the miserable resources it has in hand, tries to find an answer to the nation's great hunger and poverty.)

—Frantz Fanon

The colonized man finds his freedom in and through violence. Violence enlightens, because it indicates the means and the end. At the level of individuals, violence is a cleansing force. It frees the native from his inferiority complex. It makes him fearless and restores his self-respect.

Chapter Nine

Raw Materials

I n 1983, the young army captain Thomas Sankara seized power in Burkina Faso and started widespread reforms. He challenged both local elites and the old colonial power France. Ever since independence in 1960, Burkina Faso has been one of the poorest countries in the world, heavily dependent on foreign aid. Sankara's main objective was to make his country self-sufficient: Burkina Faso was not to accept foreign aid. Water and mineral resources were nationalized. Sankara also argued for a total cancellation of the country's foreign debt. During his four years in power he also banned female genital cutting, polygamy, and forced marriages.

After four years, Sankara was killed by his friend and colleague Blaise Compaoré, with support from France. The same fate has befallen many leaders in former French colonies when they have tried to steer away from French influence and achieve economic sovereignty. Compaoré was the president of Burkina Faso for twenty-seven years, until he was driven from power in 2014 after massive protests. Sankara's name, speeches, and ideas continue to be a driving force of protest against injustices and corruption.

—Editors' Note

CAPITALISM, IN ITS EARLY DAYS, saw in the colonies a source of raw materials which, once turned into manufactured goods, could be distributed on the European market. After a phase of accumulation of capital, capitalism has today come to modify its conception of the profit-earning capacity of a commercial enterprise. A blind domination founded on slavery is not economically speaking worthwhile.

The colonies have become a market. Today, the colonized countries' national struggle crops up in a completely new international situation.

What the factory owners and finance magnates of the mother country expect from their government is not that it should decimate the colonial peoples, but that it should safeguard their own "legitimate interests."

The private companies put pressure on their own governments at least to set up military bases, for the purpose of assuring protection of their interests. Thus there exists a sort of detached complicity between capitalism and the violent forces which blaze up in colonial territory. This is why reasonable nationalist political parties are asked to set out their claims as clearly as possible and to seek with their colonialist opposite numbers, calmly and without passion, for a solution which will take the interests of both parties into consideration. We see that if this nationalist reformist tendency—which often takes the form of a kind of caricature of trade unionism—decides to take action, it will only do so in a highly peaceful fashion, through stoppages of work in the few industries that have been set up in the towns, mass demonstrations to cheer the leaders, and the boycotting of buses or of imported commodities. All these forms of action serve at one and the same time to bring pressure to bear on the forces of colonialism and to allow the people to work off their energy.

—Frantz Fanon

Capitalism, in its early days, saw in the colonies a source of raw materials which, once turned into manufactured goods, could be distributed on the European market.

The colonies have become a market. Today, the colonized countries' national struggle crops up in a completely new international situation.

For centuries the capitalists have behaved in the underdeveloped world like nothing more than war criminals. Deportations, massacres, forced labor, and slavery have been the main methods used by capitalism to increase its wealth, its gold or diamond reserves, and to establish its power.

FOR CENTURIES THE CAPITALISTS have behaved in the underdeveloped world like nothing more than war criminals. Deportations, massacres, forced labor, and slavery have been the main methods used by capitalism to increase its wealth, its gold or diamond reserves, and to establish its power. Not long ago, Nazism transformed the whole of Europe into a veritable colony. The governments of European nations called for reparations and demanded the wealth which had been stolen from them: cultural treasures, pictures, sculptures, and stained glass have been given back to their owners.

The wealth of the imperial countries is our wealth too. Europe has stuffed herself excessively with the gold and raw materials of the colonial countries: Latin America, China, and Africa.

From all these continents, under whose eyes Europe today raises up her tower of wealth, there has flowed out for centuries toward that same Europe diamonds and oil, silk and cotton, wood and exotic products.

Europe is literally the creation of the Third World. The wealth which smothers her is that which was stolen from the underdeveloped peoples.

The well-being and the progress of Europe have been built up with the sweat and the dead bodies of Negroes, Arabs, Indians, and the Asian races. We have decided not to overlook this any longer.

—Frantz Fanon

Interview with Thomas Sankara, President of Burkina Faso, 1987

REPORTER: What is democracy?

SANKARA: I believe in the people. In the people as a strength, as a force. If you can speak to the people, if you have the people's ear, you can achieve anything. Speak to the people's hearts, so that they understand your ideas.

You need to speak about issues that people can relate to. If we talk about Star Wars, people will not know what that is. They have other worries. They want to eat, to have a place to live, to have work, health, education, roads. This is what the people understand. If you speak honestly about this, and suggest solutions, the people will listen and will put into practice those solutions or others that they come up with.

WOMAN: I am an old woman now.

SANKARA: It is when you are old that you become strong.

Our economy is indeed very weak . . . one of the weakest in Africa. We have a deficit and our foreign debts are large. But we have cut down our expenses. The bigger the expenses, the poorer we are. The fewer the needs, the richer we are.

We are reducing our needs. We are trying to get rid of all expenses based on prestige.

REPORTER LEYLA ASSAF TENGROTH: Which expenses based on prestige?

SANKARA: We are getting rid of luxury cars, for example. Our ministers fly economy class. They arrive at their destination just as quickly. This is a way of saving money. By reducing official entertainment costs and lowering salaries we have reduced our budget.

The people suffer more than we do. We must impose a minimum level of discipline on ourselves. We mustn't think that life is simple. It is simple for us, because we are state officials and have high salaries and high-status posts.

The ministers traveled to France, to Paris and sometimes to New York. These were the ministers' destinations. But now we demand that everyone should visit the farmers in the countryside, and live with them. It is very tiring and difficult. We are trying to understand their conditions, but we also realize that we have weaknesses and faults, and we are trying to educate ourselves. We are educating ourselves. We are learning English and computer skills.

TENGROTH: In order to combat desertification, tree-planting has become a priority and no event is unaccompanied without being commemorated by the planting of a tree. It could be the birth of a child, a wedding or a funeral, or, like today, an interview with the Swedish Broadcasting Company.

SANKARA: We are organizing the famers to produce food. But just production is not enough. The food must be rich and varied. We have two problems: quantity and quality. There is not much to eat. Many people eat only once a day. In your country you eat . . . more than three times a day, and still more . . .

TENGROTH: Cakes . . .

SANKARA: This is far too much!

In your country, women weigh themselves to see if they have gained weight. You make efforts to lose weight. You want as few calories as possible. We want food that will give us calories. We do not have the same problems. The weighing scale does not have the same use here as it does in your country. We want to gain weight. Out of every thousand children born in Africa, 180 die within a week of their birth. Four million out of twenty million children in Africa will die. Namely, a fifth.

It is as if you were to kill one child out of a family with five children. So you understand Africa's statistics. So if you would go to Sweden and kill one out of every five children in the maternity hospitals—there you have Africa's reality.

Women in mourning. This is their everyday reality.

Foreign financial aid must not become a miracle solution for all our problems. Financial aid is needed, but we must do the work ourselves, above all else. If you don't work, then the IMF's solutions are the easiest route. You seek help from the IMF for the smallest difficulty. That is not a good thing. But our impression is also that—as soon as help from the IMF arrives, then other conditions are imposed on us. They say: "You can get this or that amount of money, but only if you do this or that." We fulfill their conditions. Then they set other conditions.

It's very troublesome. In which countries has the IMF been successful? In which places where the IMF has meddled has it really worked? Nowhere!

TENGROTH: Can you tell me why you have said no to receiving food aid?

SANKARA: They have not helped us to develop. They have instead created a beggar mentality. We hold out our hands to receive food. That is not a good thing. Our farmers have stopped producing, because they cannot sell what they produce. The surplus from farmers in other countries is brought in here. We want something else. Those who really want to help us can give us ploughs, tractors, fertilizer, insecticide, watering cans, drills, dams. That is how we would define food aid. Those who come with wheat, millet, corn, or milk, they are not helping us. They are fattening us up like you do with geese. Stuffing them in order to be able to sell them later. . . . That is not real help.

To defend our non-dependency is a daily struggle. I do not know a single country that wholeheartedly supports Burkina Faso without demanding something in return. Only Burkina Faso can help Burkino Faso. Everyone else wants something. So this is a constant struggle. When you tell the truth, it hurts. Friends do not think you should demand things. Especially when you are a small country. But we tell it like it is. Those who try to dominate us are imperialists.

TENGROTH: If they come from the East as well?

SANKARA: If they dominate us, yes.

It is their actions that count. Not their geographical location. Not West or East.

Imperialism is a question of relationships. If you want to get to know the people here, then you are not imperialists. But if you want to get to know the people in order to dominate them, then you become an imperialist. Then it does not matter if you come from the North or the South, East or West. Not even your skin color matters then.

You can be as black as me and still want to dominate and exploit.

THEY WILL NOT MANAGE TO DIVIDE the progressive forces which mean to lead mankind toward happiness by brandishing the threat of a Third World which is rising like the tide to swallow up all Europe.

The Third World does not mean to organize a great crusade of hunger against the whole of Europe. What it expects from those who for centuries have kept it in slavery is that they will help it to rehabilitate mankind and make humanity victorious everywhere, once and for all.

The ports of Holland, the docks of Bordeaux and Liverpool were specialized in the Negro slave trade and owe their renown to millions of deported slaves. So when we hear the head of a European state declare with his hand on his heart that he must come to the aid of the poor underdeveloped peoples, we do not tremble with gratitude. Quite the contrary, we say to ourselves: "It's a just reparation which will be paid to us."

Nor will we agree to the help for underdeveloped countries being a program of "sisters of charity." This help should be the ratification of a double realization: the realization by the colonized peoples that it is their due, and the realization by the capitalist powers that in fact they must pay. But it is clear that we are not so naive as to think that this will come about with the cooperation and the goodwill of the European governments. This huge task which consists of reintroducing mankind into the world, the whole of mankind, will be carried out with the indispensable help of the European peoples, who themselves must realize that in the past they have often joined the ranks of our common masters where colonial questions were concerned. To achieve this, the European peoples must first decide to wake up and shake themselves, use their brains, and stop playing the stupid game of the Sleeping Beauty.

—Frantz Fanon

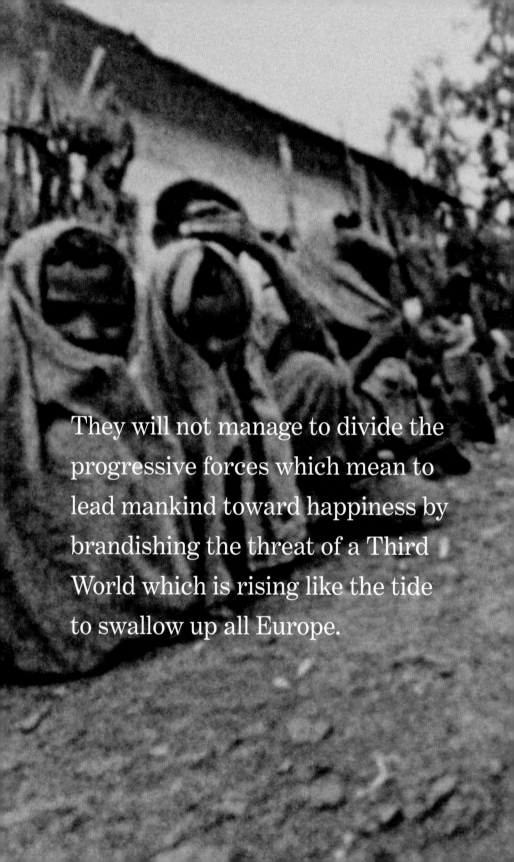

They will not manage to divide the progressive forces which mean to lead mankind toward happiness by brandishing the threat of a Third World which is rising like the tide to swallow up all Europe.

The Third World does not mean to organize a great crusade of hunger against the whole of Europe. What it expects from those who for centuries have kept it in slavery is that they will help it to rehabilitate mankind and make humanity victorious everywhere, once and for all.

THE FUNDAMENTAL DUEL, which seemed to be that between colonialism and anticolonialism, and indeed between capitalism and socialism, is already losing some of its importance. What counts today, the question which is looming on the horizon, is the need for a redistribution of wealth. Humanity must reply to this question or be shaken to pieces by it.

—Frantz Fanon

Conclusion

COME COMRADES, THE EUROPEAN GAME is finally over; we must look for something else. We can do anything today provided we do not ape Europe, provided we are not obsessed with catching up with Europe.

Europe has gained such a mad and reckless momentum that it has lost control and reason and is heading at dizzying speed towards the brink from which we would be advised to remove ourselves as quickly as possible. Europe undertook the leadership of the world with ardor, cynicism, and violence. Look at how the shadow of its palaces stretches and multiplies.

We must shake off the heavy darkness in which we were cast and leave it behind. Yet it is very true that we need a model and that we want blueprints and examples.

For many among us the European model was the most inspiring. When I search for humanity in the technique and the style of Europe, I see only a succession of negations of humanity and an avalanche of murders.

The human condition, plans for mankind, and collaboration between people in those tasks which increase the sum total of humanity are new problems, which demand true inventions. Let us decide not to imitate Europe; let us combine our muscles and our brains in a new direction. Let us try to create the whole human being, whom Europe has been incapable of bringing to triumphant birth.

Two centuries ago, a former European colony decided to catch up with Europe. It succeeded so well that the United States of America became a monster, in which the taints, the sickness, and the inhumanity of Europe have grown to appalling dimensions.

Comrades, have we not other work to do than to create a third Europe? The West saw itself as a spiritual adventure. It is in the name of the spirit, in the name of the spirit of Europe, that the West has made her encroachments, that she has justified her crimes and legitimized the slavery in which she holds four-fifths of humanity.

Yes, the European spirit has strange roots. So, comrades, let us not pay tribute to Europe by creating states, institutions, and societies which draw their inspiration from her. Humanity is waiting for something other from us. If we want to turn Africa into a new Europe, let us leave the destiny of our countries to Europeans. They will know how to do it better than the most gifted among us.

But if we want humanity to advance a step further, if we want to bring it up to a different level than that which Europe has shown, then we must invent and we must make discoveries.

For Europe, for ourselves, and for humanity, comrades, we must turn over a new leaf, we must work out new concepts and try to set afoot a new human being.

—Frantz Fanon

Europe has gained such a mad and
reckless momentum that it has lost
control and reason and is heading
at dizzying speed towards the brink
from which we would

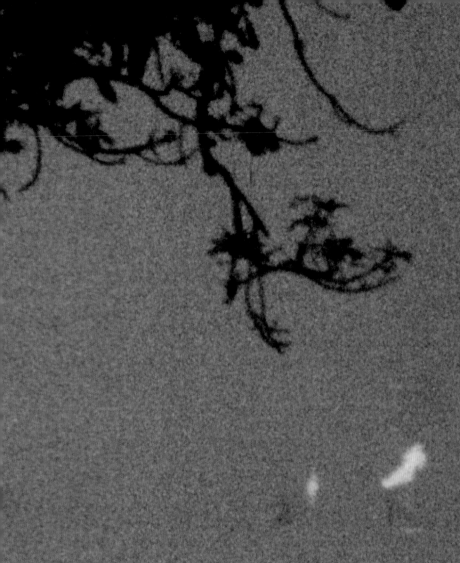

be advised to remove ourselves
as quickly as possible. Europe
undertook the leadership of the
world with ardor, cynicism, and
violence.

But if we want humanity to advance a step further, if we want to bring it up to a different level than that which Europe has shown, then we must invent and we must make discoveries.

Postscript

Dr. Görling shared the following reflections at a screening of Concerning Violence *at the Black Box in Düsseldorf on September 20, 2014.*

When I learned that you made a film on Frantz Fanon's *The Wretched of the Earth* and you named it *Concerning Violence*, I immediately was affected by the power of the title. I was not sure what it meant until I saw the film. Seeing the images, listening to Ms. Lauryn Hill reading Frantz Fanon's words, I began to realize that it has something to do with the multilayered meaning of the verb *concern*.

It is quite difficult to translate the main title into German. *Concerning*: that can mean something like referring to, you can find it on the top of a letter, abbreviated as "conc." This translates in German into *"Betreff: Betreff Gewalt."*

When you address an English letter and you don't know the name of the person who will read it, you start: "To whom it may concern" (*Sehr geehrte Damen und Herren*).

This hints at another meaning of the word. It is also used when you care about something. In German this meaning is best translated as *"Sich sorgen um, Sorge haben für."* Etymologically it derives from the Latin *concernere*, which meant in medieval times "to touch" and "to belong to." Concern is an active as well as passive form of relation. And there is a long and important religious tradition inscribed in it. This starts at least with Thomas Aquinas, it is a key word in the Methodist church, and in the twentieth century you find it in the theology of Paul Tillich and even in the philosophy of Alfred North Whitehead. Tillich speaks of the ultimate concern. We have a lot of everyday concerns—the weather, our car, our food. If necessary we would sacrifice all these everyday concerns for what Tillich calls the ultimate concern. This for Tillich is the object of faith: *Glaube*.

There is a further problem of translation: The original title is *Les damnés de la terre*. Without doubt, *The Wretched of the Earth* is not an exact translation, because the wretched are the poor, even the rogue, not exactly the damned; "wretched" has no or at least less religious meaning. But then during preparation for our talk today I learned that the first chapter in my German translation has the title "Von der Gewalt" and in the French original, "De la violence." In the English translation, it is precisely "Concerning Violence."

The title *Les damnés de la terre* had its political function in the sixties, but if one had to find a title for this book today there would be no other title as appropriate as *Concerning Violence.*

The strength of Fanon's book is that it talks about those dimensions of violence one normally doesn't want to talk about. The book is not about violence as a means, except in a very special sense that we should talk about later.

The book is about the impact of violence on all whom it comes in contact with, on the perpetrators as well as on the victims, of the impact it has on their psyche and on their bodies, on their affects and emotions, on their thoughts, their dreams, their longing. And it is about this strange fundamental concern of violence, the faith in violence, the faith of the colonized as well as of the colonizer.

This is one of the most important books to understand what is happening when violence becomes the ultimate concern of a society. We may talk about violence as a problem in the suburbs of our cities; sometimes we even talk about intimate violence in our families. But we don't want to talk about what is happening when violence has become the fundamental nothing of society.

When you talk about a fundamental nothing or no thing it is very, very difficult not to switch into religious discourse. (The important difference between Fanon's first book, *Black Skin, White Masks,* and this book is that here he uses a religious discourse quite consciously. It replaces in a way what in his first book was a literary discourse. You quote some of it: The most obvious instance is *"Die ersten werden die letzten sein"*; *"Les dernier seront les premiers."* And he adds: *"La décolonisation est la vérification de cette phrase."* The last shall be first. Decolonization is verification of this. I don't want to say that Fanon wrote a religious book. It is fundamentally political philosophy, but open to religious discourses, whereas *Black Skin,*

White Mask could be described as political philosophy open to a literary discourse.)

You all have seen the film and know that it contains many excerpts from Fanon's book. Lauryn Hill reads them with an intriguing intensity somewhere between all established forms, neither priest nor philosopher, neither teacher nor journalist, but a bit of all. But you also have music, you have the found footage, sometimes with original sound—more sound than seems to be found in the archives—and music. The relation between all this is quite complex. It comes together; you hear a narrator saying that they start shooting, you hear shooting and you see an explosion, but sometimes you have voices, sound, and pictures that are overlayed or superimposed, sometimes even in a way that one loses the sight of what side of the war we are on.

Gayatri Chakravorty Spivak says in the beginning, the film is an illustration and tribute to Fanon's book. It is not the only way I would describe the relationship. You don't illustrate; you read, comment, contextualize, and decontextualize.

And personally, perhaps it is because I have been reading this book for decades again and again, what haunts me, what recurs in my mind since I have seen this film two weeks ago for the first time are not Fanon's words but the images you show. You direct the perception of these images by Fanon's text, but I would insist that it is more than illustration.

Dr. Reinhold Görling is a professor of philosophy at the Heinrich Heine University of Düsseldorf.

Film Credits

Concerning Violence: Nine Scenes from the Anti-imperialistic Self-Defense
A film by Göran Hugo Olsson
Based on the book *The Wretched of the Earth* by Frantz Fanon, courtesy
of Editions la Découverte
Narrated by Ms. Lauryn Hill
Preface by Gayatri Chakravorty Spivak

Produced by Annika Rogell and Tobias Janson
Story edited by Michael Aaglund, Dino Jonsäter, Göran Hugo Olsson,
and Sophie Vuković
Art Direction by Stefania Malmsten
Assistant Direction by Sophie Vuković
Sound Design by Mikael Nyström
Music by Neo Muyanga
Coproduced by Joslyn Barnes and Danny Glover, Louverture Films /
Monica Hellström, Final Cut for Real / Miia Haavisto, Helsinki Fil-
mi / Otto Fagerstedt and Ingemar Persson, SVT
Associate Produced by Corey Smyth, Blacksmith Corp. / Vaughan
Giose, Rainbow Circle Film / Susan Rockefeller and Matthew
Palevsky
Final Cut for Real Executive Producers Anne Köhncke and Signe
Byrge Sørensen
Helsinki Filmi Executive Producers Aleksi Bardy and Annika Sucks-
dorff

Archival Footage

Lennart Malmer and Ingela Romare
Birth of a Nation (1974)
In Our Country the Bullets Begin to Blossom (1973)
Mozambique Is Our Country (1973)

Lennart Malmer and Pär Källberg
Poetry of Anger (1981)

Ingrid Dahlberg, Lars Hjelm, and Roland Hjelte
LAMCO: Black Week in Nimba (1966)

Bo Bjelfvenstam and Jörgen Persson
White Ants (1969)

Leyla Assaf Tengroth and Ulf Simonsson
Interview with Thomas Sankara (1987)

Lis Asklund
Interview with Tonderai Makoni (1970)

Additional Footage

Stig Holmqvist, Per Olof Karlsson, Gaetano Pagano, Alf Buhre,
    Axel Lohmann, Isidro Romero, Jean Louis Normand, Robert
    van Lierop, Lars Westman, Gudrun Schyman, Rudi Spee, Per
    Sandén, Anders Ehnmark
Jean Hermanson, Yngve Baum, Bengt Åke Kimbré, Sten Rosenlund,
    Pierre Björklund, Inge Roos, Bo Holmqvist, Sven Åsberg, Jona-
    than Dimbleby, Bo Öhlén

Archival Footage

Sveriges Television AB
INA / Office National de Radiodiffusion Télévision Française
Fremantle Media / Thames TV

Re-recording Mixer   Peter Nordström / Meguru Film Sound Oy
                          Micke Nyström

Location Sound Recordist (New York) Tammy Douglas
Grading Anders V. Christensen / Kong Gulerod Film

Research Nanushka Yeaman, Lars Bildt

Film Stills Credits

5	Lennart Malmer
24–25	Lennart Malmer
29	Gaetano Pagano
32–33	Rudi Spee
34–35	Rudi Spee
39	Yngve Baum
40–41	Tortyr
45	Per Olof Karlsson
48	Per Olof Karlsson
51	Per Olof Karlsson
52	Sten Rosenlund
53, 54–55	Pierre Björklund
59, 61, 62, 65, 66–67	Lars Hjelm
72–73	Lennart Malmer
74, 79	Jörgen Persson
80–83	Lars Westman
86–87	Rudi Spee
88–89	Rudi Spee
90–91	Stig Holmqvist
95, 96, 98, 99, 101, 102, 104	Lennart Malmer
106–7	Pär Källberg
112–15	Jean Hermansson
118–19	Sten Rosenlund
124–25	Lennart Malmer

Index of Names